What About The Bees

by

PENGUIN SCOTT

What About the Bees
Cover art by Penguin Scott

Copyright © 2023 Penguin Scott

Published by Penguin Scott / Flying Rockhopper Press Publishing
ISBN: 978-1-312-79627-0

authorpenguinscott@gmail.com
www.penguinscott.com

Dedicated to

Gary

She Lingers

Her visage was an enchanting melody of song
The kind you'd swear could keep butterflies aloft

Her hair was a misty waterfall
Cascading down her back like a leisured river
Strong enough to forge an amazing, beautiful canyon

Her eyes were pools of crystal water
A pair of deep, blue prisms with the power to pierce
the soul

Her skin was as soft silken satin
So delicately draped, uniquely exquisite

Her voice was heaven heralding me
Rendering my name as the only word that mattered
through all of time

She was the moon aglow in a dewy field of daisies

But her death was abysmal
A black hole from which nothing can ever escape

My Sister And Me

We died on the same day
my sister and me.

The tragic sense of loss
from my friends and my boss
but not from my family.

For everyone dies in twos in my clan.
Mom died the same day as our good old Aunt
Anne,
while Uncle Jim crossed over in the middle of
October
along with my dear cousin, Jann.

So it came to pass
Sister died at last
after being so ill for a week.

If only I'd known
it was my time to go.
I thought it would be dear cousin Zeke.

Sophie's Dream

Sophie's falling green tears
were her comical fears come true
Dreams of riding gondolas gave way to zebras in a balloon
Steam trains off to Buffalo where she once fell off a camel
Then riding on the dashboard of an eighty-seven Ford
With glass-like enamel

She wandered into a department store with cards and gifts
galore
Came across a table floating high up off the floor
Began eating sixty crumpets spread with pearled jam
Then to the pool deck where she spied a dancing man
Jalapeno Margarita time at happy hour in the sky
Eyeballed her mom waltzing with Dear John,
making time fly

How she busted a seam when she heard Dear John sing
Payed his tab with marbles, at the sound of the Tea Bag
cash box
ding!
And out in the distance, beyond a purple haze
She heard the conductor state the gate would shortly raise

...

What About The Bees

So pile aboard now- store your pistols and your whips
Ready your silly cow for one of those bafoonish road trips
The kind you used to take across the grand US of A
With red tape to keep you warm and bad dreams to stay
awake
Fanning your face with cards of the bad hands you were
dealt
Wound up driving side-saddle through the ludicrous rust
belt
Counting passing steeples in churches void of people
Confusing passing taxis for a yellow potato beetle

Laughing out loud above orange jello for wheels
Sophie finally knows that this is how it feels
Dreaming in a gondola and feeling rather blue
Her falling green tears were her comical fears come true

What About The Bees

Gypsies Gotta Roll

They arrive from the far corners of the sphere
Turn pleasant faces into fear
Wrapped around the treasures that they keep
Aspiring intruders, these gypsies, through the forest they
sneak
Taken from our homes the things we never find
Stuff and things we thought were left far behind
Dreams of the young and of the care free
Unspoken words seldom meant to be

They've been drunk since the 15th century at least
And they just can't settle down, the journey is their feast
Where this will end you simply can't control
But they're telling me these gypsies gotta roll

The land it takes them in, consumes their primal worth
The gypsies aspire to be the gentle lords of the earth
The wind blows and howls through the sullen trees
Gypsies hear their calling in that mystical breeze
And gather 'round an earthen fire pit's light
With rattled tambourines, twirling like embers in flight
They summon snakes, spiders, and geese
Carry on like the wolf and drink for release

...

A mythic meeting of the puma, wolf, and snake
Spirits rising from the fire to distribute astral fate
Intense fire dancing in time and in tune
She arose a green phoenix then turned to blue
Animal spirits danced with booze til the morn
Readied themselves for a painted caravan worn
To fell an evil empire in part and in whole
So glad you came, but gypsies gotta roll

Now that they're gone, heavy stillness fills the air
Phoenix feeling pained, left our spirits feeling bare
But she knows the price, we've overpaid the toll
Enlightened, deliberate, carefree, and the fun they extol
They came and went, leaving all insanely spent
You should know by now those gypsies gotta roll

Houston, Hold The Line

Worked in downtown Houston
on the 32nd floor.
It's the job that I have come to love,
the job that I adore.

I had picked up a call
doing business on the phone
I turned to look outside
when my senses all were thrown.

You would never believe this;
It's a sight you never see
Soaring through the sky
much higher than a tree.

A seven-forty-seven
was flying through the air.
I thought my sight was doubled
I thought there was a glare.

Something was atop that plane.
Yes, something on its back.
It was the NASA orbiter

...

Its grip was nothing slack.
They had come to Houston
for their final show.
In the Johnson Space Center
to reach their final home.

I watched it as it finally
flew out of my sight.
I turned then from the window
To relish such delight.

I next moved my attention
to the woman on the line.
I'm sorry for the silence
I thank you for your time.

So, What About Them

The essential preliminary findings not withstanding, certain corollary parameters have indicated a terminal breakdown of societal standards that were previously suspected to induce impending thought processes, which would seem to indicate terminal consequences to the long-range project for which we congregate at this esteemed colloquium this evening.

What with the unfortold evolution of first-cycle elements injecting virgin data into the processes of sociological constructs, many of our comprehensive first-line intuition defenders are left wondering, if general pervasive opinions from sensory deprived test subjects indicate a willingness to abandon subjective matter contained in pilot inquiries, regardless of the object-oriented programming influence on search optimized parallels, it begs the question: what about the bees?

<u>One Night Only</u>

I was drug in against my will
Never knew I'd be your prime view
Rarely knowing what's in the plan
But please
Not a one night stand

Amorous Couple

Amorous couple under yon tree
Kissy kiss
      Holding hands
      Excitement rushing
      Pants adjusting
            We all see you
            So reel it in!

Had To Pick My House

Look at the ragamuffin in his bright red truck
Seems this would-be studmuffin caught a bit of luck
Oh the excitement when his flip phone rang
To see a new call from his favorite boo thang

"Oh Mr. Studmuffin in your bright red truck
Please come on over, please come and pick me up
Let's go to your place, so we can get it on
There are too many fire ants to do it on the lawn"

"Sorry babe, my folks are home and I'm feeling ike a
louse
We'll just have to park in front of someone else's
house"
So the studmuffin wannabe picked his boo thang up
Now the two of them are doing it inside his bright
red truck

Scene On A Friday Night

Not a half-bad job, you sure can parallel park
On a Friday night, pissing in the dark
Was it just a random pass or have you been on
scout
Watched you very carefully as your tools were
soon brought out
Ferry across the street: so desolate and quiet
Back into your car with your license plated diet
Smile for the camera, your fame surely awaits
Friday night out driving and stealing license plates

No Need To Worry

I worried about you so
when the world crashed
But then I realized
you fell off the planet long ago

Now In Haiku:

I worried for you
when the world came to an end
but you left it first

The Cemetery Of Willowside

There are headstones in the tiny cemetery at the corner of
Willowside.
Simple headstones made for creatures who have recently
died.

Headstones at the base of a tree that grows near a wooden
fence.
Means of death not mentioned: not why, not how... just
whence.

A handful of headstones, in a cemetery so small and nice.
Pay close attention, I hear they dish great mystic advice.

The cemetery cues that in gratefulness, all should heartily
imbibe
So find those headstones in the shaded grass at the corner
of Willowside.

Eagle On Stony Point Road

Eagle on Stony Point Road
In a tree under which we strode
Sitting atop twisted branches
Rodents hide; taking few chances

Eagle looking down on me
From high up his favorite tree
That road up on Stony Point
The eagle's necessities now conjoint

Eagle at rest under a clear blue sky
Perch a bit longer and soon you'll fly
Appearing so regal, emphatically bold
A memory this day magnificent to hold

Betty By The River

Betty by the river
Steely by blue
Good times to deliver
Her worries are few

Betty is sleek
Tender and kind
She has a mystique
Elegance refined

She'll take you out
To reel you in
Cast no doubt
Take a spin

Betty, sweet bug
What you do to me
Gives my heart a tug
To the river we shall flee

A Little Beach Graffiti

A little beach graffiti
On a wall along the sand
Aged wood pylons
Splintered where they stand

A stroll along the waters
Lapping at our feet
Passing by a cyclist
Young woman on the seat

Feel the Gulf shore winds
Ruffling at your hair
Enjoy the coastal evening
To the surf is where you stare

And there below the boardwalk
Painted on a fence
Spray can as the medium
Insightful and intense

A little beach graffiti
I wonder what it means
Like a foreign language
Only seen in dreams

Vine Creeping Over The Back Fence

Vine seen creeping over the back fence
Creeping and peaking o'er the back yard fence
Leaves of green with a spider web sheen
Flowers so white they could light up the night
Vine spiraling round now the fence be
crowned
Seen here creeping with leaves well heaping
Vines all over the back yard fence
Crawling upwards so fresh so dense

> Beauty galore
>
> Hard to ignore
>
> Fence is prime
>
> Sublime climb

Vine seen creeping...over the back fence

Hello, You Robin

Robin stopped to say hello
As he sat up on the fence
Waiting for the wind to blow
Then to flight he did dispense
True he'd flown for quite some mile
Yes he'd flown so high
Sure was nice to see him smile
And then I waved goodbye

In The Back Yard

One of the jade plants is blooming
Right in our own back yard
After a summer of water and grooming
The jade is looking avant garde
Five star pedals done up in pink
Look how they reach for the sky   .
Hope they'll stick around- not gone in a wink
I'd sure hate to tell them goodbye

A Bowl Of Lemons

Lemons in the morning sun
A bowl-full of yellow
Their taste cannot be outdone
Their fragrance far from mellow
Centerpiece on table run
A flavorful bordello
So now the day has just begun
This lemon-rooted bellow

Rotocraft

Helicopter whirlybird
    My attention ensnared
        Blades spinning around
            Chopping through the air

        Hovering there
    Perfectly still
Away you go
    Such a thrill

        Helicopter whirlybird
           Way up in the sky
                Wish I were up there
                    With you I'd love
                      to fly

Staff

The power of the staff is something to behold. Just hear the cries of those under its priapic spell. Head held high. Confidence. Glow. Fire. The power of the staff both feared and admired. Wielded for good and the power will proliferate. Used for nefarious purposes and worlds can drain into nothing, the sorcerer left barred and scarred. The power of the staff is something to behold.

Juniyel

Your lives are present in your eyes
A magnificent beast powerful in the night
It was but a dream

I drove my car across a frozen ocean chasing you
Afraid of breaking through
Sluggish because of the ice under the tires cracking

I sailed a ship over the body of a continent zig-zagging
Where rippled dessert sands whisper and deceive
At last, in a sandbar just off shore, catching me

Behold the eyes that hold so much curiosity
The setting morning sun blinding me
I toss

Sand in my eyes rubbed away like specks on the screen of
my phone
I laughed when you jumped surprised
After waking you from dreams of your lives

Again laughing because whiskers tickle

Festival Of Mythos

Then suddenly it became so clear
She is the woman of the year
Whose broken free of hefty bonds
And won't sit still for very long

No longer fear she's running from
A new day's tide has just begun
Deep within the soul is screamin'
A transformation from a demon

And then she's gone without a word
A myth hence forth that oft be heard
When long from now folklore bespoken
They cheer of how the spell was broken

Then myths of bewitching crystal invention
Will entertain all with composed intention
Ribbons of black with bows seen hanging
Hypnotic hearts and kettledrums banging

People come to hear this story
Cheer the myth's uplifting glory
Singing praises revere her name

Inspire long her implicit flame
To this we'll feast with family together
Then gifts exchanged wrapped in leather
To represent her wondrous spectacle
That now festoons this yearly festival

Protectress

The one I love the most
Is the one who hurts equally
Internally burned when the truth offends
Sees my faults all too clear
Thinking I'm often too silly
Or sometimes dense
And knows the fire within me is fear

And I run to her whenever I can
For she keeps a light burning for me
She helps my sight remain focused
Attends to that which could trip me
Or catch my toe
A light that only few can see

Should I ever go out of my mind
She stands in my way
With her soft hand reaching out
She keeps me on the path of good
I would go it alone
But I don't think I could

Protection Spell

Dark ribbons of energy
Seep from the ocean blue
Come from the far reaches of space
Spiraling around
Healing intentions abound
Bright embers of light
Like sparks shower down
Dancing around
Are here to help
Night and day
Keeping harm far, far away

Healing Energy

Falling through the air, this rain that hits the ground
Splish splash rain from the sky makes such a healing sound.
The rain is falling everywhere the rain is falling down.
These are not a rain of tears but rain of healers, in this rain we wish to drown.
We'll take the rain that heals, we'll take all the vibes you'll send.
To be strong and rebound in the end.
I ask the gods to hear my prayers, a quick recovery and well health to attend.
I ask this for my loved ones. I ask this for my friends

<u>Potion</u>

She ties her sacred knots discretely
Waves her broom high in the air
Her silver knife thrust in her cup
She is like Venus in her lair

Walking with the Lunar Lady
Who anciently wanders the land
She gives to us everything
In return takes only our hand

Justified in knowing her ways
She calls upon the radiant Lady
Intent to set the wheels in motion
With hopes for me her sugar baby

She casts her spell of cunning intention
Waiting for it to land on me
Soon I see her shapely visions
Nightly in my repeating dream

At last I walk a lover's daze
Out of sorts and oddly confused
Blindly I trace a path unwilled
She's fervently awaiting, giddy and bemused

What About The Bees

Open Road

Enough for today no further can I go
The road that led me here is but clear
One day to this town I go
The next day another, I drear
The roads leave me astray
I'm so far from home, so far away
Another time another life
Time to dine in a truck stop tourist shop
Leaving little change on a Formica table
Catching TV on the motel cable
Well, look at me
Lying at the bottom of an open-road sea

Bridge Crash Backup

Bridge crash backup
All lanes are full of cars
Just a touch of bad luck
Traffic reaching far

Just ahead a fender bender
Hope everyone's OK
Such gridlock I can't remember
Since the one the other day

Come on, already, move that wreck
I'm running awfully late
I don't mean them disrespect
Let's not enter a debate

This stop and go has got me blue
Why can't we all just go?
Move aside and let me through
Please let this traffic flow

Bridge crash backup
Slow movement across the bay
Just behind this Mack truck
Been here half the day

Public Transportation

Crusties at a bus stop on San Pablo Avenue
I wonder where they're all going
Are they together? Along with those 2 mutts?
I'll have to live never knowing
Upon which route is their bus

I see them stand with their instruments
Wile driving past twenty-two sixty
It would be so grand if they were in a band
Ladies and gentlemen, the Bohemian Pixies

Stay Strong

Turgid thoughts
Lucid and cavalier
As a battle rages within
Pricey and callous
Flighty and austere
So you run for your pillow
and blankets

You might as well, now
For the sun is obscured by
clouds
And rain splashes down
Until the second day
Then you progressively awake
And throw this grief down

That fist clenched in your chest
Kept you from breathing
Clean, clear, and organic

Speech that escaped you was
silent necessity

...

Laughing turned to maniacal panic
And with one degree of separation
Delight can be newly obtained
Starting fresh with a stronger game
Inside us grow rings only found
After we've been cut down
But we'll have no feelings left
By then

Betrayal

I see in the faces of friends
Secrets kept from me by you
Blather is garish
My enemies run deep
Your trap soon falls into view

Cracks dawn in your twisted coup
Down the hallway whispers flap
Shadows crossing light
Barely visible under the door
Before I leave this trap
I rip and tear the décor

I am not the only soul broken
Or to float in your fountain of fear
The smoke screen you crafted
In light all lambasted
Seemingly innocent, my dear

With feet firmly planted
Wrapping us up in your dark
Your profound absence of tact
We're broken, hurt, and wracked
To say nothing of the wounded hearts

Ahead Of His Times

I lit a candle for a boy I know
Who ran before he wheeled
And laughed per chance to heal
His pen hushed was such a devastating blow

    How sweetly a poster child dreams
    So then brightly his smile beams
    In writing poetry he inspired many
    And kept the world full of hope
    Winning over hearts aplenty
    All within a body that couldn't cope

And now a dog lies alone
At the end of a lonely hall
Waiting for the day this boy comes home
But the boy never really left at all

    Let us to the moon our hearts to moor
    We'll search the world from shore to shore
    In hopes that one day
    We may finally find his cure

        ...For Mattie Stepanek

You Left Too Soon

Alone in a room full of people
A planet of my very own
A world all to myself

Then you walked in

I am the flower
I am the butterfly

I am the one left behind to cry

Voice

Uh oh, I'm in trouble again
An invisible voice is telling me so
Is it the trouble I fear or the voice itself
It doesn't matter whichever the case
The two are one
All I know is that I'm in trouble now

It's a voice I once knew
I'd come to hear all through my life
The rest of it I've left far behind
Hoping the memory will fade
I know it never will
Voice makes certain of that

Voice knows when something isn't working
out
Saying give it up and leave it far behind
Voice is taking me home
Home home home and then I will be free
Voice feels much like home to me

I'm afraid
I'm frightened of home to me

Perspective

Not sure why I do, but I feel miffed when people use their phones on speaker in public spaces. I'm unsure if it's due to finding it annoying that someone thinks I am interested enough to hear their disquieting discourse; that the conversation isn't entertaining enough to hold my interest; or that the lunk is too lazy to hold the infernal phone up to their ears. Regardless, I was recently obliged to pay witness to a conversation while in a waiting area.

A woman was around the corner in conversation with her daughter. From the live voice and the careful timing of phrases, complete with pauses in order to recall words necessary, I ascertained that she was elderly. After establishing the fact that she was still at her appointment, she asked the lady on the other end if she could come pick her up. Daughter, sounding flustered by the way she inflected, "Mommmm." asked Mom if she didn't already *have* a ride. Before Mom replied, Inside Voice said, Well, she wouldn't be asking *you* for a ride if she had one now, would she? When Mom said she did have one, Inside voice said, You should have lied. Mom told Daughter it would take an hour before Ride would arrive. Her daughter could be there in 10. I appreciated Mom saying it would take an hour. Nothing like a Texas Tall Tale to make your point. Daughter wasn't having it.

...

When the conversation was complete, the woman revealed herself to me as she crossed the waiting area to make her slow exit. She was in her 80s and on a walker. It was one of those fancy walkers with a little basket and a fold-down seat, in candy apple red, new tires and an estimated top speed of 1 MPH with a tailwind. Undercoat is extra.

I excused her use of the speaker phone. At least she was able to use a smart phone. My own grandmother couldn't use one, saying it was smarter than she was. Truthfully, it was her arthritic fingers that made it difficult. My grandmother was smart as a steel trap. This lady was very grandmotherly and took her daughters indignation more comfortably than mine would have. But to have the audacity to interrupt her daughter for a ride? Take half an hour of Daughter's day to play taxi with Mom? Come on, woman. Priorities.

When my appointment was over, walking to my car, there was Mom, sitting on her walker at the primary entrance. Money well spent, to be sure. I had a feeling that fold-down seat got used plenty. I approached with a smile, amazed that she was still waiting. Not sure why—it had been an hour (so much for Texas Tall Tales). Subsequent to a pleasant exchange, I inquired where she lived, and it wasn't entirely distant in a different direction from my destination, but I had nothing else to do. I was nigh to offer a ride when she said hers would be there any minute now, and it would be a bother to call and cancel this far into her wait. It was a delightful day, she seemed satisfied, reposed in her seat, and didn't appear to be in a good deal of distress.

As I walked to my car, I felt so sorry for her. Not for Mom, but Daughter. One day in the not too distant future, she won't have her mother around any more. And might she and I be akin, my kingdom for the chance to spend 20 minutes transporting my mom home. Or my grandmother, for that much. It's funny how losing your mother alters your perspective on life; deepening the little moments of time spent with loved ones. The small potatoes that appear to be a bother no longer are, in retrospect. But in retrospect, it's too late.

Desire V Reality

Watching out the window but careful of being
seen
Sweet dreams appear to her, filling a deep ravine
She plots her way back to a time in her past
Closing her eyes to remember, memories fade so
fast
He must be out there somewhere, never was he a
blur
Of this she's very certain, and is definitely sure
And the one that he is searching for is someone
just like her
Wandering long in search of an undefined allure

Whispers, "Everyone I see is molded from you….
The moon and sun are doings only you can do."
When you hear her laugh you can practically hear
his name
She's hopeful his presence will forever change her
game

In the rafters of some desire, he is standing there
In the realm of reality, he stands but nowhere
She falls into the sky and surveys the view
Says, "I'm slowly losing hope of ever finding you."
He must be walking circles without a single sound
But for in her foolish mind, never may he be found

She dreams each every sleep that she can see it all
In the light of day she takes a heavy fall
Left in the balance is what she thinks she feels
Against what she reckons simply must be real
Where will she ever go, where has she ever been
Nightly sheds a tear and once more cries out for him
A universe of dreams is reality's certain loss
She might up and die should their paths ever cross

What About The Bees

He Is The Fool

Something grips at his throat
When she comes near
Something grips at his heart
When she goes away

The heart quickens
Hardens then dies
He slips down
Come or go
And it bores me to death

He enters the spiral
At breakneck speeds
And floats with
The greatest of ease
She draws near

Floating down
Falling below the ground
He is the fool
She fades

    Waiting and waiting
    He will flounder
    In a sea
    Of mental breakdowns
    And emotional take downs

A Silence Is Coming

One of the hardest things
Is realizing I must let you go
One of the best things
I've ever done
Is doing just so

I had fallen so hard
I had felled a creep

There once was a connection
Like no other
It's still visible in the garbage heap

New destruction has run its course
And the pain is forever deep
So I withdraw where once I came to life
A lesson learned that was not cheap

Two steps forward
One step back
Reinvent myself
Reinvent my needs

I withdraw from you
A silence is coming
I won't be here long
So say what you need

Sky For One

Wasting away under a sky for one
Absent of clouds and devoid of sun
I long to see the night

For the stars once more take flight
For this hardship journey to evolve undone
As I succumb under a sky for one

Set up for hurt your encouraging word
The meaning of which to me is blurred
I feel it's cruel- what you intend to be kind
To free my spirit, hopelessly confined
You are besotted, on your intentions I'm hung
As I languish under a sky for one

With so many others the sky I share
But their tribulations I do not care
Such strife I stave and I endure
Perpetually endless a pretentious cure
Singularly attended to be tallied among
Existing afflicted under a sky for one

<u>Not Again</u>

No more songs to write
They have all been written true
And the saddest songs are all about you
They have all been written before
Falling in love, staying together, breaking up, moving on
A voice soft as chiffon
And I yawn
If I do one more round on the dance floor
I will forfeit my senses more than I have so often before

Depleted

The song I play may not restore the best feelings I ever felt
The pictures pull at my heart like a hit below the belt
The moisture on my face won't be tracks from the tears of joy
My feelings at night lend to curl into a ball, as if a little boy
The fruit I eat will not be very sweet
My company reflected by those who might entreat
The words I write may bring me to my knees
They will not be very kind nor of the sort to please
The time hereafter passes not as when having fun
The bags I keep packed are for being on the run
The bird outside my window may be the black bird of death
The breeze coursing my dejected body likens a dove's final breath
Broken and defeated I'm feeling depleted over you

Sad

I am the saddest man in the world
I can feel the life drain from me
Running to escape

My well of pain overflows
I cry out...only my breath empties

The crashing of my heart breaking fills my
ears
Roaming within my head and taking root

I'm not functioning right
Messing up
Patience is gone
I scream at strangers
        I scream at myself
                I scream in a vacuum
Nothing gets completed

Abysmal is the void I infest
So cold is the once productive spirit

I'm the casing of the majesty I was before
For I am the saddest man in the world

Settle

I'm sorry I don't have the swimmer's body
That you love so much
Or the looks of a god
Nor do I have the charms to keep you engaged
I cannot be the man you want to love
For the rest of your life

When you came along
I was stuck in the mud
You offered your hand to help me out
All I can do now
Is circle around atop the wall you've put up between us

I look down
Deep and wide
Barely able see the other side
Overwhelmingly strong
A fortress true
To breech these walls would be wrong
The role I've played time and again can be no more
You only want a friend
I wanted to be your only man
Guess I'll settle for whatever I can

In Fields Of A Distant Plain

No more time for pleasure
No more time for pain
This life that's thrust upon me
Has created a man insane

No more smiles of pleasure
No more tears from pain
I'm full of nothing over which
Sanity should be reigned

Now that the sunset is so complete
And the water has receded from the shore
Turn your gaze away from me
You may worry yourself no more

No more use for pleasure
No more use for pain
I've freed myself unbound to run
In virgin fields of a distant plain

<u>So The World</u>

The skies are so grey all over the world.
Clouds consume it in whole, not just above *me* unfurled.
No sun,

      no stars,

            no moon,

                  nothing in tune.
Only clouds above the entirety of Earth are strewn.

I can barely remember the day that the skies above me
were clear.
All I can see, high into the sky, is a consuming
      blanket of fear.

Time was so long ago when everywhere,
everything we know seemed to be right.
No darkness of night,

      no shadows,

            no clouds,

                  nothing but light.

I'm thinking, surely soon the rain will begin.
I have no place to go when the rain turns to snow and the
cold makes my skin feel so thin.

It matters not if it is snow
           falling from the sky or if it is rain.
No matter what falls from the heavens above nothing is
           felt but a loathing bane.

I may climb a mountain to get closer to the clouds and find
out what lies within.

But the lack of the sun means soon night is begun; and the
           bleakness of night will begin.
At least the blackness of night with its absence of light,
makes the grey skies seem ever contrite.

Until that time, the sky will stay grey most every day...
now that the clouds have moved in.

What's Left Behind

When my eyes close forever
You may understand how I feel
What I mean
How it was
All the reasons
Soon to realize
     I see,

          hear,

               feel,

                    cry
In sleep I know all the reasons why
I know only in sleep
And it keeps me in good trouble
Stretching for something just out of reach
Things that left me a long time ago
When I close my eyes forever
You're eyes will finally be open,
     clear,

          red,

               sheer
And wish you'd done more
When I was still here

Wearing A Mask

You say the things
That I want to hear
   Build me up

Your smile is only a mask
Your intentions
Have become crystal clear
   See me fall

You sink into a darkness
Of the kind I never
Knew could exist
   Crash and burn

You have a catalog
Of dark deeds
You favor to score
   Dash my hopes

You possess profound beauty
But only on the outside
   Reveal my fears

...

You have such wickedness
Lurking just beneath
   Hold on tight

Build me up
   See me fall
      Crash and burn
         Dash my hopes
            Reveal my fears
            Hold on tight

Fill Me With Rain

At night when I can't sleep
I walk the streets
For mental therapy
People's pace quickens
When the rain starts to fall
Not mine
The rain cleanses me, fills me
Builds excitement within me
Helps me focus
Keeps my feet on the ground
A rainy night is made for walking

Back Again

I exchanged inspiration
For an arm chair and a six pack
I traded vision
For melancholy
I swapped knowledge
For a numbing view of a lifeless sea

I extinguished the light
That was to illuminate my path
Because deep inside of me the desire died
Driving the light from my days

I know well the solitude
Of an island at sea
Because the cause and reason in my life
Has been so distanced from me

But I do not cry
I do not fret
Nor will I flee
I will simply stay the course
In search of my next
Reason to be

I Want To Be

I want to be a Muslim
Because we are feared the most
To be of faith so misunderstood
Vilified from coast to coast
Oh, I want to be a Muslim
Of this I wish to boast

I want to be Mexican
Because we are trusted least
To be the sort who comes to stay
And pilfers our union's feast
Oh, I want to be Mexican
My value's now decreased

I want to be African-American
Because we've nothing left to lose
To live in ghettos while bullets fly by
While neighborhoods unwillingly defused
Oh, I want to be African-American
And keep singing up the blues

...

I want to be the handicapped
Because we are mimicked and mocked
To be put down just to bring you up
Our ingress always blocked
Oh, I want to be the handicapped
With issues to be teased and gawked

I want to be a queer-American
For the ungodly things we do
Cast out because of who we love
Recoloring the hatred that they spew
Oh, I want to be a queer-American
With false agendas forced on you

I want to be a woman
Because we are the weaker sex
To be belittled and coddled
Your manhood to be vexed
Oh, I want to be a woman
For my pussy lacks respect

I want to be Hillary
So mistrusted and so feared
To be witch-hunted all my life
My gifts so little cheered
Oh, I want to be Madam secretary
My name so falsely smeared

I want to be these and more
Often belittled and put down
To believe the fears the blind dish out
Seemingly heralded as their crown
Oh, to be all things the intolerant fear
To bury oppression below the ground

Let us rise and speak of tricky things
Festering from untouched fears
Once bigotry is cleared from the slate
Hypocrisy's screams are snubbed from ears
And when hatred's grip can only hold honor
We'll live the Shangri-La in open-minded frontiers
It is in this spirit we wipe out hate
As the true road to make our nation great

Faith In The Blind

I'll do as I do and not as I say
I will hate this and I'll hate that, even as I pray
The flag I fly may inspire great pain
A concept I keep shielded from my minuscule
brain
Ultra conservative ways leave very little room
So minds can stay dark and nicely entombed

We cling to our past and shun what comes
next
As long as it's written in clear Bible text
Take what we need and align, as required
To contrive a new meaning that we so desire
Using key words and symbols and signs
To keep us together within our own kind

We'll meet and smile and eat and shake hands
And conspire to send others back to their
home lands
We don't want inclusion, we don't want to
grow
We only love that, which already we know
No facts will dissuade us from what we
believe
We're faithfully blind and blindingly naive

Puppet

I am a lonely puppet
Whose strings are quite attached
My movement is often rugged
My thoughts are all unlatched

Little thought is ever given
When strings are pulled by others
No need to craft a wise decision
No need for many colors

From the day that I was born
To the day that I shall die
From freedom I'll be torn
From freedom I will shy

I am a puppet- see my strings
Don't feel so bad for me
I'd never trade them in for wings
I see no need to flee

Said Is Said

Under the surface
Lie scars of your past statements
That are unseen.
Facing them drives panic.

There is much you wish to convey
Dissuaded when facing the end result,
If you even had that kind of strength,
There is more comfort in keeping things as
they are,
Yet you sense failure.

You implore for objects stolen by time never to
return,
Instead, hoping to find the good they once
represented.
Even if you could bring them back,
You might die waiting.

Things will never be that way again-
Everything changes
Words tend to remain

<u>Song</u>

The world came crashing down
I sang a song
Mothers were out in the street
And I sang a song
The world came flaming around me
So I sang, yet I felt so hollow

Brothers take to arms
Marching up the street
And all I could do was sing
Sisters twitching so
You'll get back to the scene you know
And we'll sing from the inside to the outside
world
And fill within us what became hollow

And tears might fall
If not for our feelings
Then for the sadness in our voice
I'll turn the other cheek for only so long

Will wait only as much as I have to
Which means I'm here until the end
Adding my voice of song to express
Inspiration
Strength
Demonstration
Empowerment
Celebration
Peace
Motivation
To memorialize
For healing

To carve a path forward
I will sing a song like none other
Like in days of old
When a lifted voice cleansed painful wounds
With poetic words and lofty tunes
Let us come together and sing a song

Pebbles

Such dark visions that impose on my mind from not far enough away. They were unfamiliar and did not affect my day.

But they would affect my life. And they have clenched my world.

His name was George Floyd, and he died with a knee upon his neck. And that vision of death circles my head like an ad flickering and flashing in peripheral sight, most annoying and unkind. It infects my life.

Being scared of the blue is something that to me is strikingly new.

Not for George.

That day he fought with his fears clearly on display for a stunned world that so suddenly shrunk. He struggled with the reality that was his, and his kind, for a very long time. He wasn't different. He was human.

He was laid upon the ground with a knee upon his neck. The struggle was real.

Just breathe.

Respiration is not cheap. He can't afford it this time. He can't afford it this day. Breath is not free when forced to the ground; and there is that knee.

That knee upon his neck.

He cries out for his mother. She has always been there when needed. But not this time; too far away. He calls out for his brothers. Come quick. Help! They've had is back before. But not this time.

There is a single knee upon his neck.

The pavement, with innumerable puny pebbles, that together create a behemoth, that day were only tiny pebbles. He had never noticed them. Yet each one invaluable. No one sees the road for the pebbles. Things look different close up and near death. From a distance they seem solid. But up close, with a careful eye, one can see each

little

part

that makes up a whole. No. Not George. He wasn't allowed to make it whole...wasn't allowed to BE whole. The road that day—a behemoth—became his cage. He was but a paltry pebble, with a knee upon his neck.

The pavement grew dark and the breathing narrowed. There was a wooziness filling...all-consuming.

It was the darkness of his eyes closing that consumed him as he fought to breathe. His mind wandered and flashed.

...

The Cuney homes; the skyline of Houston; the Third
Ward...now but sudden flashes in his mind.
Schooldays.
Family dinners.
Doctor visits.
Riding the bus.
Crying a tear.
Laughing a laugh.
Sighing a sigh.
Breathing a breath.
Flashes. Flashes. Flashes.
His last, final, breath. And that **knee**.
His fade into darkness complete, and he is gone.
George departed with a knee upon his neck. No
resuscitation. No Mama. No brothers. No chance to live
free.
He died,
but so much came to life
the day the world learned his name...George Floyd. A
pebble in the road. A road we've traveled down. A road
we must follow. A road with strength, character, laughter,
tears...life...but a road nonetheless. A road not unlike
George, a behemoth made of innumerable pebbles.
Forever ours-- with a knee upon his neck.

Forever

Don't be bothered by the lilies and their
desire to be more grand. Until we
make the lilies understand
that white is white
and white is bland
we'll have to simply let them be. They're a flower
forever and never a tree. So when you're
next at a funeral or flower show,
talk to the lilies and let them know that they can
think, wish, and dream. They're forever
a flower,
so it would seem.

And Ever

The people of late have approached
the lilies as they stand. Tell them
not to attempt to be
more grand. They are white
flowers and that is bland, but to
wish for more is poppycock. Judge them
not for the strength of
their stalk. Judge them
more for the power of thought.
Because the people who
approach to squash their dreams,
are still only people and not
kings and queens.

Star

His whole life he wished to be a star, floating around in the heavens. Bright and high with adoring eyes ascending. But the enigma of being a star is loneliness. Floating around in the heavens distanced from all; it only appears on the outside their proximity to others. To discover how each star is viewed by only a few when not neglected in the day sky.

So plentiful are they... who really notices a single one? Even established constellations manage to keep hidden the names of their stars from curious minds but for a few fanatics.

The stars cry united and their tears fall long; their pain unobservable. The stars cry through our day and night and as they grow and become bright, approaching their dwarf, they soon will die.

All his life he wanted to be a star, floating around in the heavens so high.

All his life he was blind to reality. All his life, he was a star all along.

Song Of Night

Carried away on a sea of lullabies
Is this voice for real?
                    Be not lies
          The chorus
The waves
The darkness that welcomes a tired soul after long and
tiring days

Sing to me a verse that soothes
Sing this starry night
For he, for she, the old, and youths
Help me sleep good and tight

                    To dream
          To see
To scheme
To feel a part of the greater whole when it's only me

Hold me tight in covers tucked
Hold me tight in slumber
With tasty dreams upon which to sup
In hues of violet and umber
Morning comes soon, but first comes the night

With the Sandman's sand gathered for bleary eyes
But first, please sing soft, as soft as the sprite
Spanning across the dark, on delicate seas of lullabies

Zapp Airmail

Missouri River flows
Misty dreams floating by
Fill my lungs
Fill my pride
Filled my mind til the end of time
Let me float down
Softly like music
Swimming in my mind
A river dammed six times

The end of the street
Curves like a spine
In a field of green
I can't tell if it's a spaceship
Or maybe just three pies
It means everything
It's the universe of a young boy's mind

Grimsrud, save us!
It's Zapp Airmail
Our Orange Spaceman
He always delivers
Flying high

Til the end of time
Taking me to places
Trepidation supposedly erases

Never knew who it was dedicated to
Says it was back in 1972
A centennial celebration
Absent holiday hesitation
Dedicated to me
From you
From your lips
On the Missouri River shores
Lift off from the grassy ellipse

It was a messed up plan
Something I'd never understand
I would run
To a star
So far away
It would rise
In an unfamiliar sky
Bringing tears to my eye
Goodbye Zapp Airmail
Our orange spaceman

What About The Bees

Daydream

I dream that I am floating
I dream of your syrupy face
I dream all the colors of winning a race

I dream we are dancing
At the imperial ball
And dream I am floating away from it all

Then I come to, all soaking wet
Drenched in perspiration, my hair
a visual threat
(As is my ever drifting mindset)
I breathe in order to breathe
dreams in
And dream that I am breathing
through a dream fin

I sleep through the entire day
It seems I sleep the sun astray
I feel like I am swimming
But going upstream
Life is but a pillowy daydream
Floating me away

She Remembers Everyone

I saw her in the local store
A shy boy, that was me
I spied her while shopping
She was a star of stage and screen
Finally I approached
My heart I think it skipped a beat
I asked her to film another movie
She winked and then placed an order for meat
Many years later we would meet again
By now I'd had my own taste of fame
But of course she remembered me
For Greta Garbo was her name

Catching Fish

Catch them in the deep 900 feet or more
Catch them past the reef and bring them all ashore
Whether in a power boat or one with a sail
Catching villagers dinner- with nets you cannot
fail
Some fish brightly colored are terrible to consume
And if not prepared just right may impart certain
doom
The fishing is much better when caught beyond
the reef
Some fish are much smaller we'll return them back
to sea
Our limit caught our day is done our time was
such a treat
We thank the gods for all the fish that we're about
to eat

What About The Bees

Finding Her

Gotta take it slow
Heart's not what he used to be
Feeling a little hollow
Or something, I don't know
I'll find some sane remedy soon
Maybe someone to hold me up
To keep me angry or keep me down
I know who, but...
She'll want to read the new writing in my
book again
However, I can't recall the movement of my
pen
It's stuck
This heat makes me melt
So I need someone to stay
Follow my lead
Write the way
Through the night into the day
And then I'll be off again

Kingdom Of Dust

Marble halls and
Marble walls
Matter not here.
A woman calls
Wrapped in shawls
Seeking survival gear.

She's a tired old bone
On an empty throne
And so approaches dusk.
Sets a dark tone of
Desires full grown
In her kingdom of dust.

Her subjects all lost
She knows the cost
Of ruling them all alone.
She floats across
Her walls of moss
And of crumbling stone.

Empty halls and
Barren walls
Are all that she can see.
No one calls,
No army falls
No leaves on the tree.

What is this?
I see her lips
Curl in an upward way.
She blows a kiss
To what she's missed
And is eager to say:

I'm a fool
For powers that rule
And satisfies my lust.
I think it not cruel
I continue to rule
Here in my kingdom of dust.

Hofflindinker's Distinctive Pointed Hat

Little Hofflindinker on a mushroom sat
Wearing his distinctive pointed hat
And from the tip of his hat what did fell
Than the jingle of his tiny silver bell
Such a spectacle did he never see
When hearing his little jingle flee

He jumped up quick to search for that jingle sound
That had dropped from atop his hat to the ground
He looked aplenty with all of his skills applied
Just where the hell did that jingle hide?
It is not something that you can see
The sound of a jingle is a challenge to perceive
To find it requires the use of one's ears
But doing so could take quite a few years

Thus the aid of his friend, a witch, he did seek
Who appeared in an instant at his feet
She laughed when she heard Hofflindinker's tale
Then pulled from in her robes a dragon's scale
A powder did rest in this scale of a bowl
Which the witch then poured... all out whole

What About The Bees

The ground next began to wiggle and shake
Hofflindinker thought the whole world might break
But this is not all these two chums did hear
For the tinkle of the jingle, too, was near
Acting quick, the witch clutched at the sound
Then both delighted that the bell's jingle was found
The witch held on tight as she gave it back
To be restored to the bell of Hofflindinker's hat

So the bell and its jingle were together once more
Yet there was a conundrum Hofflindinker wished not to
ignore
What's to prevent this from reoccurring, he asked the
witch
And she replied, "You merely need a magical stitch"

She took the distinctive pointed hat from his head
And revealed that she had some invisible thread
She stitched real quick and soon was done
Then said to Hofflindinker, "I must run
It's growing cold and I have no cloak"
And with a wave was gone in a puff of smoke

Little Hofflindinker put his bell to the test
He shook it and heard it jingle its best
He returned to his head his distinctive pointed hat
Once more on his mushroom Little Hofflindinker sat

Sinister Penguin

Something is felt deep inside
He'll say anything…nothing to hide
After all the promises kept
To find you guilty and inept
He is completely sinister
A downright tricky minister

It's another log on the fire
The static of telephone wire
In your mind his soul will reign
And old ladies start talking to rain
You've got something of a wonderful talent
Does that make you any more gallant

Camera lenses full of action
The curtain falls on a premier attraction
Some days of old still cast in blue
In second story windows are scenes of youth
Never thought you'd be asking for more
Thought you'd never get through the door

Keep alert for his fiercely rogue crew
Draws them out then sends all askew

A stellar mix he's forever spinning
Bird's got skills so prizewinning
Forget what's in front you, better look behind
That sinister penguin will blow your mind

Sing

Another night alone
I get tired of so many in a row
Your face fading in my hands
Fragile hands forgetting love
Forgetting strength

Knowing the fragile state of my heart
I will die...
One day I will
Don't let it be alone
Don't let it be still

With you by my side
The world is busy
The tastes are richer
The drink intoxicates
The song binds our soul

So stand with me
Together let us sing
Together we can grow old
Together we will live forever
Alone I fade away

I feel cold
I long for the fire you bring
I feel lonely
I long for my soul to sing
Your song gives me hope

I don't know what to do
If I can't sing with you
My hero
My everything
With you I will have...
The best years of our life

<u>Compass</u>

I came here not so long ago
From so far away
And the only hand to guide me
Was that of the North Star

    I needed something
    But what
    Absent clues, I'd learn along the way

        West is where I was led
        But I couldn't tell you why
        I got there and nothing was right
        Not in me nor in the others I met

            But then came the day
            I could see me in the reflections of you
            When looking at your shadow from the
            sun
            So I decided to stay

Return To Winona

Moving my way back to LA
How these senses commence to fray
That road has so many meandering twists
Although it ends with Winona's honeyed kiss
Since taking me there
I return for that impassioned affair
Trapped ever so sweet in her amorous snare

Winona like a beloved syndrome
Designs to make this my eternal home
But those erotic flames
Transforming into a refreshing game
I'm thinking about Winona every day
Exploring virgin ambitions for which to splay

She's greater than a rainbow in the sky
I falter and presume to deny
Should insanity be my penultimate act
Know my fantasies she has certainly cracked
Provided I pull through to that seductive zone
Delight in achieving a victory full-blown
Retreat me near to my dear Winona

...

Winona, glorious ethereal beam
Temptress unravel this euphoric scream
Entreat to that mountainous dream

Akin to an astronomical scope
Seeking a mystical tactile trope
Ever clueless to impressions on this broken man
Disseminating her devious, wanton plan
Speed along before my sight becomes hazy
That trembling touch lest my mind turn crazy
Uncertain of which desires to pursue
Winona's demand, a sensuous cue
Dispatching boundless bewitchment askew
Must get back to LA for Winona

Back In LA

Over a plate of pad se ew
Was our first date
A duet played strings so true
The view was splendid
Brown eyes that never let me down
Heart sounding a steady beat
Skin began to feel the heat
Brushes in hand we would paint the town
A wheel way up high
Blackened our sky
But never kept us from going out
It was a magazine cover story
Told first hand
News piled high across the land
Hollywood Avenue kept dry
Terrific distractions and me elope
The glimmer flashed in your eye
Took me down firsthand
Without hope
I smiled wide

White Noise

I may be Elio
Scared and haunted
New and discreet

I remember it all
Visions of gray and white
Savored delusions to pleat

In the middle of summer
A snow fallen day
Visions only seen
By the light of a dream

Played lucky enough
To have met
Danced
And kissed
Blinded by the emotions
Of our secretive tryst

The mystery of love
All bitter and sweet
A midnight foray
I kindly entreat

I am the heavens
Planted deep within you
Aching to be free
When I am with you
All the world is me

Peony

My honey is an argosy
Supplies me with delight
Casts me in a shadow
Couldn't stand the light
Better bring your pillows
Soft purple and creamy white

My honey is an argosy
Helped save my life
One day sent a card to me
The first one and the last
Wishes of prosperity
Before this ship was cast

Gathered up my very best
Lush and showy friends
Dressed me up in honesty
Peonies to extend
Unsure where this argosy
Would take us in the end

My honey is an argosy
Gold purple creamy white

Supplied in rich prosperity
Driving through the night
Peonies lined the highway
Think they saved my life

My honey is an argosy
Gave me lots of love
Fascinating history
Singing turtledove
Sweet smells in the air stream
Were never quite a dream
Peonies down the highway
Purple, gold and cream

Places And You

I'm on top of the Eiffel Tower
Drinking hot chocolate along the Seine
Dancing through a Parisian shower
A genuine champagne dream
It doesn't thrill me
Quite the way you do

I'm in the heart of the Big Apple
Broadway lighting up the night sky
Skyscrapers cutting like architectural scalpels
Dining on deli corned beef on rye
It doesn't excite or amuse me
Quite the way you do

If found in Japan sipping miso soup
Or on the China Wall admiring how it sprawls
I could be under London on the Tube
Or soaking in the mists of Niagara Falls
Nothing arouses my interest
Quite the way you do

All of the cities and many great places
Quite a few that I've seen
All of the extraordinary faces
Are ordinary and routine
For nothing fascinates or revs me up
Quite the way you do

In Love

You are my garden
I feed off the love you give

You are my soil
Through you I grow

You are the water rising from the depths
and falling from the sky
My thirst is quenched

You are the air
I breathe in deeply

You are the stars
So that I find my way
though the night

APPENDIX OF POEMS
And background information
Cover art by Penguin Scott on the road in the Canary Islands

*   These poems were inspired by the photography of Bruce Wismer, a friend who often posts photos with the kind of captions that call for having a poem written. Most of the titles here are those captions. A single photo and a single caption was all I needed. Most were written between 2014 and 2016.

38 **Open Road** written in 1997 when living in Annapolis.

39 **Bridge Crash Backup*** is one of my favorites from Bruce's photos.

40 **Public Transportation*** was originally titled *Bus Stop Crusties*.

41 **Stay Strong** was written 1988 when in college.

43 **Betrayal** written in 1997 about life events from the 80s.

44 **Ahead of His Times** was written in 2003 when finding out Mattie Stepanek had died. I knew Mattie from my days as GM of the Harley business. He was the MD spokesperson who wrote poems and invigorated me to keep writing in the late 90s. He was a good friend.

45 **You Left Too Soon** is pretty much the story of my life: waiting too long to go say hello. Written in 1994 at the tail end of my acting days.

46 **Voice** written in 1996.

47 **Perspective** a true tale written in 2023 while working on this book.

50 **Desire V Reality** written in 1995.

52 **He is the Fool** from 1999, after watching a friend be overly dramatic at a breakup that needed to happen.

54 **A Silence is Coming** written in 1999. Probably from the same friend.

56 **Sky For One** an old poem from 1988 on which I got an A.

57 **Not Again** written in 2019 after becoming single again.

58 **Depleted** was written in 1996.

59 **Sad** inspired from a photo I took in S. Korea in 2009 of a woman, head in hand.

60 **Settle** also from 2009. A true tale.

61 **In Fields of a Distant Plain** is from my time in Maryland in the late 90s.

62 **So the World** Muse inspired in 2014. One of my favorites, and I wan't feeling low when I wrote it.

64 **What's Left Behind** is another from my prolific period in 1997.

65 **Wearing A Mask** In 1997, I'd write late into the early morning drunk.

67 **Fill Me With Rain** written in 2005.

68 **Back Again** written in 2013.

69 **I Want to Be** written in 2016 based on current events. I grew tired of the groups that make up the fabric of America constantly being belittled.Keeping it as originally written was a conscious decision.

72 **Faith in the Blind** written during the tumuluous political climate of 2016.

74 **Puppet** certainly not autobiographical, if you know me. Written 2017.

75 **Said is Said** written in 1995 about regretting things said in the past.

76 **Song** about the power of our collective voice written 2000.

78 **Pebbles** what can I say about this that the poem doesn't? During the march held in Houston, at one point I noticed how the road was made up of tiny pebbles. Such small things independent of each other, but so strong together.

81 **Forever** I found this in my pile of poetry notes dated 2006. I wrote the following poem as a follow up to this one because I felt it needed that voice in response.

82 **And Ever** 2023 in response to the above.

83 **Star** written 2009 about a friend who longed to be more than he was, but I thought he already was.

84 **Song of Night** written while at the University of Houston, 1988.

Other works by Penguin Scott:

◊ **"Upon the Hues of Sunset"** – A little more philosophical, with poetry on heartbreak, as well as uplifting works on travel and falling in love.

◊ **"Dragonflies Surrender"** – More personal poems that touch on family, relationships, Burning Man, and the arts.

Coming soon:

Penguin's, "Travel Lust" a series of novels about his travels as a flight attendant.

ABOUT THE AUTHOR

Penguin Scott was born and raised in Texas. He grew up in Houston and moved between there and Dallas several times. He began writing poetry in high school when he lived in Dallas. Penguin didn't get serious about poetry until college in the late 1980s, at the University of Houston, where he studied creative writing. He would eventually live on all three US coasts.

During the early and mid 1990s, Penguin joined the performance company at the Texas Renaissance Festival in Houston. This period of creativity encouraged him to hone the writing talents he developed in college.

In 1995 he moved to Annapolis, MD when purchasing a Harley-Davidson dealership with his father. He credits this difficult period of his life, being away from family and the stress of working alongside his father, as being the inspiration for one of his most prolific periods of writing. It was during this period he earned the nickname Penguin, based on his collection of penguin items—at one time the largest collection in the USA.

In 2000, Penguin left Annapolis for San Francisco, taking a job with a major airline. His travel lust spawned many travel poems during the 2000s. Living in the San Francisco Bay Area for 14 years introduced him to various artistic influences. He attended Burning Man, the world's largest outdoor arts festival and showcase for radical self-expression, for seven years (2001 to 2007).

This led to an expanded social circle of fellow "burners," a cohesive and colorful group of friends who would come together for monthly camp outs on the beach, for what was essentially 48-hour raves with a bent on artistic creativity. Many poems were written on this beach, and an area known as The Jungle.

In 2014, Penguin transferred and moved back to Texas to spend time caring for his maternal grandmother. Considered the leading ladies of his life, she and Penguin's mother were among his biggest fans of his writing and poetry, encouraging his expanding talents.

In 2017, Penguin rediscovered his poetry notes, that when combined, formed a stack of papers over a foot high. He began pouring through them to cull his favorites and flesh out some that were unfinished. The collection showcased in this series of three books, released in 2023, are only a small portion of what he has written since the mid 1980s. Surely, more will follow.

In the span of five years, Penguin lost his father, mother and grandmother, as well as several dear friends and other family. Additionally, he contracted the Corona Virus in December, 2020, and is still struggling with Post Covid conditions that affects his cognitive skills, preventing him from fulfilling his role as a safety a professional with the airline. At least temporarily.

If you've enjoyed this book, please buy more copies—they make great gifts. If you wish to purchase an autographed copy or donate to the PenguinScott Post Covid Fund, contact him directly. Penguin Scott accepts Paypal donations at the email address below.

Penguin Scott can be reached as indicated here:

penguinscott.com
authorpenguinscott@gmail.com